FAITH'S LITTLE INSTRUCTION BOOK II

More Supercharged Quotes To Blast Doubt Out Of Your Life!

Harrison House, Inc.
Tulsa, Oklahoma

Faith's Little Instruction Book II:
More Supercharged Quotes To Blast Doubt Out of Your Life!
ISBN 0-89274-826-5

P.O. Box 35035
Tulsa, Oklahoma 74153

Introduction

Faith's Little Instruction Book II is a unique collection of powerful, faith-building quotes from leading Spirit-filled men and women of past and present. These quotes, coupled with Scriptures, will strengthen and encourage you to stand firm and trust in the promises of God.

Based upon the best selling *Faith's Little Instruction Book I*, this little book will challenge you to do more than stand by and watch things happen. It will move you into action to put God's Word into practice in your life. These quotes will stir your spirit as you read from Kenneth E. Hagin, Kenneth Copeland, Gloria Copeland, Smith Wigglesworth, Benny Hinn, T.D. Jakes, Paul Crouch, Kathryn Kuhlman, Creflo Dollar, Jr., and many others.

This book is a treasure of wisdom from some of the greatest people of faith in our times, but more importantly, it is a treasury of the timeless wisdom and guidance of the Bible. *Faith's Little Instruction Book II* was designed to be a burst of hope and inspiration – we pray that it is in your life!

God will dare to do the impossible in your life if you dare to step across the faith line!

Kenneth Copeland

... Our God whom we serve is able to deliver us from the burning fiery furnace, and he will deliver us out of thine hand, O king. But if not, ... we will not serve thy gods ....

Daniel 3:17-18

God delights to allow these impossible situations to prove HIS mighty power to deliver.

Paul F. Crouch, Sr.

You are my help and my deliverer, O LORD, do not delay.

Psalm 70:5

. . . .When we cut ourselves off from every other help, we have never found the Lord Jesus Christ to fail.

John G. Lake

By faith Abraham, when called to go to a place he would later receive as his inheritance, obeyed and went, even though he did not know where he was going.

Hebrews 11:8 NIV

Only those who can see the invisible can do the impossible.

John Avanzini

By faith the walls of Jericho fell down, after they had been encircled for seven days.

Hebrews 11:30 NAS

You may trust the Lord too little, but you can never trust Him too much.

Benny Hinn

Trust in the Lord with all thine heart.

Proverbs 3:5a

As long as God is on His throne and hears and answers prayer, and your faith in Him is intact, everything, everything, everything is going to be alright.

Kathryn Kuhlman

Come unto me, all ye that labour and are heavy laden, and I will give you rest.

Matthew 11:28

Real faith in God simply says about one's self what the Word says.

Kenneth E. Hagin

And God raised us up with Christ and seated us with him in the heavenly realms in Christ Jesus . . . .

Ephesians 2:6 NIV

Often it is the small, almost insignificant things that ultimately determine our destiny.

Paul F. Crouch, Sr.

. . .If you have faith as small as a mustard seed, you can say to this mountain, 'Move from here to there' and it will move. Nothing will be impossible for you.

Matthew 17:20-21 NIV

Faith is comprised of three things:

1. Facts to be believed,
2. Commands to be obeyed, and
3. Promises to be enjoyed.

A. E. Mellors

In God, whose word I praise, [in] God I have put my trust; I shall not be afraid. What can mere man do to me?

Psalm 56:4 NAS

Before you can affect the world out there, you have to overcome [inside yourself] in here.

Buddy Harrison

To he who overcomes and does my will to the end, I will give authority over the nations. . . .

Revelation 2:26 NIV

Living by faith is not something you try. It's a lifestyle.

Kenneth Copeland

. . . Shadrach, Meshach and Abednego . . . were willing to give up their lives rather than serve or worship any god except their own God.

Daniel 3:28b NIV

Don't call it like it is. Call it the way . . . God promised.

Charles Capps

And my God will liberally supply . . . your every need according to His riches in glory in Christ Jesus.

Philippinas 4:19 AMP

Faith is the only thing in this world where there is true equal opportunity.

T. D. Jakes

I am not ashamed of the gospel, because it is the power of God for the salvation of everyone who believes: first for the Jew, then for the Gentile.

Romans 1:16 NIV

Acting on reason instead of relying on God's Word means to trust in the arm of man instead of God's Word.

Kenneth E. Hagin

[Paul said, . . .] We. . . worship by the Spirit of God . . . and put no confidence in the flesh–though I myself have reason for such confidence.

Philippians 3:3-4 NIV

. . . Faith is like a bulldog that has finally found the bone of its wildest dreams! . . . He is going to stand by that bone and never, ever relinquish it.

Rick Renner

. . . Jacob said, I will not let You go unless You declare a blessing upon me . . . And [the Angel of God declared] a blessing on [Jacob] there.

Genesis 32:26b, 29b AMP

Faith is a requirement, not an option.

Myles Munroe

. . . For the just shall live by faith.

Galatians 3:11b

[The power of the Holy Spirit] fills you with the boldness and stamina you need to stand against the negative tides . . . of sickness, fear, . . . poverty, loneliness, and family disruptions.

Oral Roberts

For David . . .
said, 'The LORD
says to my Lord:
Sit at my right
hand until I make
your enemies a foot-
stool for your feet.'

Acts 2:34-35 NIV

Once love is ruling, the Word is working in us, and faith becomes a dominating creative force. . . Then we can reach out and help others.

Pat Harrison

All the believers were one in heart and mind. . . . they shared everything they had. . . . There were no needy persons among them.
Acts 4:32-34a NIV

God is orchestrating and ordaining your steps and your life–if you are yielded to Him.

Carlton Pearson

I will lead the blind by ways they have not known, along unfamiliar paths I will guide them. . . .

Isaiah 42:16a NIV

Faith will deteriorate where there is continual sin without repentance.

Billy Joe Daugherty

If we confess our sins, he is faithful and just to forgive us our sins, and to cleanse us from all unrighteousness.

I John 1:9

It's okay to ask God for something you've already seen Him do; but He wants to do more . . . .

Myles Munroe

Now unto Him that is able to do exceeding abundantly above all that we ask or think . . . .

Ephesians 3:20a NIV

Faith is more
than a fact.
Faith is an action.

T. D. Jakes

*. . . Then he said
to the paralytic–
"Rise, take your bed,
and go home."
And he rose
and went home.*

Matthew 9:6-7 NAS

Prosperity is your ability to use God's ability.

Jim Zirkle

. . . Do not be anxious [beforehand] how you shall reply in defense or what you are to say. For the Holy Spirit will teach you in that very hour and moment what [you] ought to say.

Luke 12:11-12 AMP

Take a faith stand, then refuse to let the devil talk to you about that situation anymore.

Jesse Duplantis

Resist [your enemy the devil], standing firm in the faith . . . .

I Peter 5:9 NIV

Remember, something GOOD is going to happen to you.

Oral Roberts

So I will always remind you of these things, even though you know them . . . .

2 Peter 1:12a

The great need is not to *do* things, but to *believe* things.

Oswald Chambers

. . .According to your faith be it unto you.

Matthew 9:29

Real faith is both a fight and a rest.

Billy Joe Daugherty

And whatsoever is born of God overcometh the world: and this is the victory that overcometh the world, even our faith.

I John 5:4

Stop looking at where
you have been,
and start looking at
where you are going.

Mike Murdock

Jesus said to him,
No one who puts
his hand to the plow
and looks back
[to the things
behind] is fit for
the kingdom of God.

Luke 9:62 AMP

True faith is always in Someone–in Jesus, in what He said, is saying, and in what he is doing.

Reinhard Bonnke

This righteousness from God comes through faith in Jesus Christ to all who believe.

Romans 3:22 NIV

You must be willing to go where you have never been, to create something you have never had.

Mike Murdock

The Lord had said to Abram, "Leave your country, your people and your father's household and go to the land I will show you. . .and I will bless you. . . ."

Genesis 12:1-2 NIV

To have fear is to lack faith in God.

Benny Hinn

And He said unto them, "Why are ye so fearful? How is it that ye have no faith?"

Mark 4:40

Never be afraid to trust an unknown future to a known God.

Anonymous

The LORD is good,
a refuge in times
of trouble. He cares
for those who
trust in him.

Nahum 1:7 RSV

God always gives His best to those who leave the choice with Him.

Jim Elliot

If the LORD is pleased with us, he will lead us into that land, a land flowing with milk and honey, and will give it to us.

Numbers 14:8 NIV

God writes with a pen that never blots, speaks with a tongue that never slips, and acts with a hand that never fails.

Anonymous

Let us hold unswervingly to the hope we profess, for he who promised is faithful.

Hebrews 10:23 NIV

Real, active faith . . . is what is expressed in the beautiful deeds and actions out among the people who are in need.

Daisy Osborn

. . . It was right and commendable and noble of you to contribute for my needs and to share my difficulties with me.

Philippians 4:14 AMP

The beginning of anxiety is the end of faith, and the beginning of true faith is the end of anxiety.

George Mueller

. . . Take up the shield of faith, with which you can extinguish all the flaming arrows of the evil one.

Ephesians 6:16 NIV

A righteous person is a positive, faith producing person who is actively pursuing a God-given dream.

Robert Schuller

. . . We have put our hope in the living God, who is the Savior of all men, and especially of those who believe.

I Timothy 4:10 NIV

Faith . . .
brings into our . . .
hearts a spiritual force
greater than our
circumstance.

Charles Capps

Truly, truly, I say to you, he who believes in Me, the works that I do shall he do also; and greater works than these shall he do; because I go to the Father.

John 14:12 NAS

The evidence that we want victory is our pursuit of praise.

Rod Parsley

Believe in the Lord your God, so shall ye be established. . . . Praise the Lord . . . .

2 Chronicles 20:20-21

Some people fail to recognize opportunity because it so often comes to them in overalls and looks like work.

Anonymous

For we are His workmanship, created in Christ Jesus for good works, which God prepared beforehand, that we should walk in them.

Ephesians 2:10 NAS

God puts no restriction on faith; faith puts no restriction on God.

John L. Mason

. . . If our hearts do not condemn us, we have confidence before God and receive from him anything we ask. . . .

I John 3:21-22a NIV

Faith is spelled R-I-S-K!

Robert Schuller

. . . So faith without deeds is dead.

James 2:26 NIV

Faith works by love. Love gives and forgives. So faith can't operate without love.

Buddy Harrison

. . . If I have a faith that can move mountains, but have not love, I am nothing.

I Corinthians 13:2b NIV

A Christian has a reason for his hope, and a hope for his reason.

Anonymous

Through him you believe in God . . . and so your faith and hope are in God.

I Peter 1:21 NIV

Faith is the audacity that rejoices in the fact that God cannot break His own Word.

Smith Wigglesworth

And all things, whatsoever ye shall ask in prayer, believing, ye shall believe.

Matthew 21:22

The presence of your faith is proved by something you do in obedience to God and His Word.

Mike Murdock

Here is the perseverance of the saints who keep the commandments of God and their faith in Jesus.

Revelation 14:12
NAS

We are to live by faith because the Word of God commands us to live that way.

Jerry Savelle

. . . As it is written, "But the righteous man shall live by faith."

Romans 1:17 NAS

When you have nothing left but God, then for the first time you become aware that God is enough.

Maude Royden

Taking the five loaves and the two fish . . . .they all ate and were satisfied, and the disciples picked up twelve basketfuls of broken pieces that were left over.

Matthew 9:16-17 NIV

Faith is the tongue by which we taste how good the Lord is . . . .

George Mueller

O taste and see that the LORD is good: blessed is the man that trusteth in him.

Psalm 34:8

Faith, like light, should always be simple and unbending. . . .

Martin Luther

For through the Spirit, by faith, we wait for the hope of righteousness.

Galatians 5:5 RSV

Confess abundance in the face of apparent lack.

Charles Capps

I can do all things through Him who strengthens me.

Philippians 4:13 NAS

You will always live to the level of your faith.

Edwin Louis Cole

. . . The righteousness of God is revealed from faith to faith . . . .

Romans 1:17a NAS

Unbelief demands . . . material evidence rather than faith.

Ray McCauley

Jesus said to him, Because you have seen Me, Thomas, do you now believe? . . .Blessed . . . are those who have never seen Me, and yet have believed. . . .

John 20:29 AMP

Effective faith demands a lifestyle in which you abandon yourself to the Bible.

Creflo Dollar, Jr.

This book of the law shall not depart from your mouth, but you shall meditate on it day and night, so that you may be careful to do according to all that is written in it; for then you will make your way prosperous, and then you will have success.

Joshua 1:8 NAS

Faith works with hope –intense expectation!

Kenneth Copeland

The things which are impossible with men are possible with God.

Luke 18:27

There is an attitude of faith that makes it possible to live in the midst of trouble without being troubled.

Jerry Savelle

Thou will keep him in perfect peace, whose mind is stayed on thee: because he trusteth in thee.

Isaiah 26:3

Faith will turn every defeat into victory. It is God's formula!

Gloria Copeland

Be not afraid or dismayed at this great multitude; for the battle is not yours but God's.

2 Chronicles 20:15b AMP

All it takes to receive from God is a little bit of faith in a great big God.

Kenneth Hagin, Jr.

You shall not need to fight in this battle; take your position, stand still, and see the deliverance of the Lord [Who is] with you. . . .

2 Chronicles 20:17a AMP

Feed your faith, and your doubts will starve to death.

Anonymous

*Fear not, nor be dismayed;
tomorrow go out against them, for the Lord is with you.*

2 Chronicles 20:17b AMP

Patience is the battery that runs the clock of faith.

John Avanzini

I waited patiently for the LORD; and he inclined unto me, and heard my cry.

Psalm 40:1

. . . The life of faith is an heirloom that must be passed on from one generation to another.

Jerry Savelle

. . . Do not forget the things your eyes have seen or let them slip from your heart as long as you live. Teach them to your children and to their children after them.

Deuteronomy 4:9 NIV

The readiness to take risks is our grasp on faith.

John L. Mason

Without faith it is impossible to please him. For whoever would draw near to God must believe that he exists and that he rewards those who seek him.

Hebrews 11:6 RSV

As human faith gives birth to . . . achievements in the natural realm, so the believer's faith in the Father and His Word gives birth to spiritual achievements.

E. W. Kenyon

The Lord sets prisoners free, the Lord gives sight to the blind, the Lord lifts up those who are bowed down . . . .

Psalm 146:7b-8 NIV

Love keeps faith from becoming selfish because love always reaches outward either to God or man.

Billy Joe Daugherty

. . .With humility of mind let each of you regard one another as more important than himself; do not merely look out for your own personal interests, but also for the interests of others.

Philippians 2:3b-4
NAS

Dare to believe it, and God will perform a miracle for every setback along the way.

Benson Idahosa

. . . Rest assured, brethren, that what [has happened] to me [this imprisonment,] has actually . . . served to advance and give a renewed impetus to the [spreading of the] . . . Gospel.

Philippians 1:12 AMP

Faith does not make things easy–it makes them possible.

Anonymous

He rescued me from my powerful enemy, from my foes, who were too strong for me.

2 Samuel 22:17-18 NIV

A doubter often prays for things he already possesses.

T. L. Osborn

Watch out! Be on your guard against all kinds of greed; a man's life does not consist in the abundance of his possessions.

Luke 12:14 NIV

Give your troubles to God; He will be up all night anyway.

Anonymous

Humble yourselves therefore under the mighty hand of God; that he may exalt you in due time; Casting all your care upon him; for he careth for you.

I Peter 5:6-7

Faith in God means you can have faith in others . . . .

Daisy Osborn

Then Jonathan said to David, "Whatever you say, I will do for you." . . . Jonathan made a covenant with the house of David . . . .

I Samuel 20:4, 16
NAS

The thing that moves God is faith.

T. D. Jakes

For the eyes of the Lord run to and fro throughout the whole earth, to show himself strong in the behalf of them whose heart is perfect toward him.

2 Chronicles 16:9a

Everything is possible if you will abandon yourself to an idea enough that you are willing to lose your life for it.

Myles Munroe

He that findeth his life shall lose it: and he that loseth his life for my sake shall find it.

Matthew 10:39

Faith is believing God more than we believe our feelings, more than our apprehensions.

Reinhard Bonnke

There is no fear in love–dread does not exist; but full-grown . . . love turns fear out of doors and expels every trace of terror!

I John 4:18a AMP

Praise is the language of faith.

Kenneth Hagin, Jr.

Praise be to the Lord God, the God of Israel, who alone does marvelous deeds.

Psalm 72:18 NIV

Keep your foot on the devil's neck by standing on the Word of God, and you will see tremendous results!

Jesse Duplantis

. . . And this is the victory that overcometh the world, even our faith.

1 John 5:4

If you want anything from God, you will have to pray into heaven. That is where it all is.

Smith Wigglesworth

For if any of you lacks wisdom, let him ask of God, who gives to all men generously and without reproach, and it will be given to him. But let him ask in faith without any doubting . . . .

James 1:5-6 NAS

. . . When God tells you to make a step of faith, He has a plan and a reward in mind.

R. W. Schambach

For truly, I say to you, if you have faith as a grain of mustard seed, you will say to this mountain, 'Move from here to there,' and it will move; and nothing will be impossible to you.

Matthew 17:20 RSV

. . .The Word . . . must be reality to you–more real than the problem you face.

Terri Pearsons

Then Jesus said to his disciples: "Therefore I tell you, do not worry about your life, what you will eat; or about your body, what you will wear. . . . Do not be afraid . . . ."

Luke 12:22, 32a NIV

Preach faith until you have it.

John Wesley

. . . Grow in the grace and knowledge of our Lord and Savior Jesus Christ.

2 Peter 3:18a NAS

Don't be afraid to take a big step. You can't jump a chasm in two small jumps.

David Lloyd George

Jesus said unto him, if thou canst believe, all things are possible to him that believeth.

Mark 9:23

Faith does not deny fact; it changes it.

Benny Hinn

And He said to them, "...if you have faith as a mustard seed, you shall say to this mountain, 'Move from here to there,' and it shall move; and nothing shall be impossible to you.

Matthew 17:20 NAS

If you really are in faith, . . . you will know that in the spiritual realm you have it and all you are doing is waiting for it to manifest in the physical realm.

Ray McCauley

For we walk by faith, not by sight.

2 Corinthians 5:7

God doesn't work on *maybe's*. God works for *believers*.

Norvel Hayes

But let him ask in faith, nothing wavering.

James 1:6a

Expectancy is the atmosphere for miracles.

Edwin Louis Cole

And God did unusual and extraordinary miracles by the hands of Paul, [so] that handkerchiefs or towels or aprons which had touched his skin were carried away and put upon the sick, and their diseases left them . . . .

Acts 19:11-12 AMP

. . . Faith doesn't come from the Name [of Jesus]. Faith comes from hearing and hearing by the Word.

Kenneth Copeland

So then faith cometh by hearing, and hearing by the word of God.

Romans 10:17

. . . Be faithful [to walk] in those [revelations] God has already given you.

Gloria Copeland

Whoever can be trusted with very little can also be trusted with much . . . .

Luke 16:10a NIV

Faith is daring the soul to go beyond what the eyes can see.

E. C. McKenzie

Now faith is being sure of what we hope for and certain of what we do not see.

Hebrews 11:1 NIV

We believe the Word of God; therefore we do the Word of God.

Frederick K. C. Price

. . . I will show you my faith by what I do.

James 2:18b NIV

Rising above mediocrity never just happens; it is always a result of faith combined with works.

John L. Mason

Even so faith, if it hath not works, is dead, being alone.

James 2:17

Faith produces a very positive attitude.

Jerry Savelle

For whatever is born of God overcomes the world; and this is the victory that has overcome the world–our faith.

I John 5:4 NAS

Faith comes from knowing more of God everyday.

Albert Hibbert

. . . I consider everything a loss compared to the surpassing greatness of knowing Christ Jesus my Lord . . . .

Philippians 3:8 NIV

You must be willing to do the ridiculous if you ever want the miraculous.

Patricia Avanzini

By faith Noah,
when warned about
things not yet seen,
in holy fear built
an ark to save
his family.

Hebrews 11:7a NIV

Faith . . . is just letting God do what He says He will do.

Reinhard Bonnke

And let the peace of Christ rule in your hearts. . . and be thankful.

Colossians 3:15 NAS

Great faith is the product of great fights.

Smith Wigglesworth

Then David said to the Philistine, You come to me with a sword, a spear, and a javelin; but I come to you in the name of the Lord of hosts, the God of the ranks of Israel, Whom you have defied.

I Samuel 17:45 AMP

Faith . . . [and] patience. . . have to be joined together to be truly effective.

Creflo Dollar, Jr.

I waited patiently for the Lord; [and] He inclined to me and heard my cry . . . .Many will see and fear, [and] will trust in the Lord.

Psalm 40:1-3b NAS

Faith heals, sets free, receives from God, and walks in liberty.

Ray McCauley

It is for freedom that Christ has set us free. Stand firm, then, and do not let yourselves be burdened again by a yoke of slavery.

Galatians 5:1 NIV

Faith . . . comes from hearing and acting on the Word that specifically deals with that particular need.

Creflo Dollar, Jr.

For I know that this shall turn out for my deliverance through your prayers and the provision of the Spirit of Jesus Christ.

Philippians 1:19 NAS

Our profession of faith . . . is the way we act and talk continuously.

Kenneth Copeland

. . . As God's chosen people, holy and dearly loved, clothe yourselves with compassion, kindness, humility, gentleness and patience.

Colossians 3:12 NIV

The highest purpose for faith is not to change my circumstances but to change me.

Anonymous

In all this Job sinned not, nor charged God foolishly. . . . In all this did not Job sin with his lips.

Job 1:22, 2:10b

You simply need to use the faith you have by taking God at His Word and acting on it.

Kenneth Hagin, Jr.

Consider my affliction and deliver me, for I do not forget Your law. Plead my cause and redeem me, revive me and give me life according to Your word.

Psalm 119:154 AMP

Sorrow looks back.
Worry looks around.
Faith looks up.

Anonymous

Rejoice in the Lord always; again I will say, rejoice! . . . The Lord is near. Be anxious for nothing . . . .

Philippians 4:4-6a NAS

. . . Trust in God, and you are never to be confounded in time or eternity.

Anonymous

To you, O Lord, I lift up my soul; in you I trust, O my God. . . . No one whose hope is in you will ever be put to shame . . . .

Psalm 25:1-3a NIV

Faith is simply bringing what is invisible into visibility.

Frederick K. C. Price

Then Moses stretched out his hand over the sea, and all that night the Lord drove the sea back with a strong east wind and turned it into dry land . . . and the Israelites went through the sea on dry ground . . . .

Exodus 14:21-22 NIV

One individual with faith and action constitutes a majority.

John L. Mason

Then Samson prayed to the Lord,. . . "Let me die with the Philistines!" Then he pushed with all his might, and down came the temple on the rulers and all the people in it.

Judges 16:28-30a
NIV

Brethren, be great believers. . . . Great faith will bring heaven to your souls.

Charles Spurgeon

But the Angel of the Lord called to [Abraham] from Heaven, . . . Do not lay your hand on the lad, or do anything to him; for now I know that you fear and revere God, since you have not held back from Me or begrudged giving Me your son, your only son.

Genesis 22:11-12 AMP

Faith is not belief without proof, but trust without reservation.

Anonymous

My eyes are ever toward the Lord, for He will pluck my feet out of the net.

Psalm 25:15 AMP

Your heart is like a treasury . . . You make deposits into your heart by hearing the Word.

Jerry Savelle

Lay not up for yourselves treasures upon earth. . . .
But lay up for yourselves treasures in heaven . . . .
For where your treasure is, there will your heart be also.

Matthew 6:19-21

Faith is the seed of healing.

Gloria Copeland

And the prayer [that is] of faith will save him that is sick, and the Lord will restore him; and if he has committed sins, he will be forgiven.

James 5:15 AMP

Seed faith is the system that God depends on to assure the propogation of every life form He created on Earth.

John Avanzini

[Remember] this: . . . he who sows generously and that blessings may come to someone, will also reap generously and with blessings.

II Corinthians 9:6b AMP

Don't just talk faith in a good confession, but begin to act upon your confession

Bill Basansky

. . . Joshua said to the people, Shout; for the Lord has given you the city . . . . They raised a great shout, and [Jericho's] wall fell down in its place, so that the [Israelites] . . . took the city.

Joshua 6:16, 20b AMP

When God moves, when you feel the rustling of His Spirit, you had better move with Him, or you'll move on your own.

R. W. Schambach

. . . for it is God who is at work in you, both to will and to work for His good pleasure.

Philippians 2:13 NAS

Faith will create an attitude that will enable you to have peace that passes all understanding.

Jerry Savelle

Be careful for nothing; but in every thing by prayer and supplication with thanksgiving let your requests be made known unto God. And the peace of God, which passeth all understanding, shall keep your hearts and minds through Christ Jesus.

Philippians 4:6-7

If you will diligently seek any blessing you find in the Word of God, it will reward you by manifesting.

John Osteen

[My word] shall not return to Me empty, [without] accomplishing what I desire, [and] without succeeding in the matter for which I sent it.

Isaiah 55:11 NAS

Keep your faith by maintaining a relationship with God . . . .

Lester Sumrall

. . . I count all things to be loss in view of the surpassing value of knowing Christ Jesus my Lord, for whom I have suffered the loss of all things, and count them but rubbish in order that I may gain Christ . . . .

Philippians 3:8 NAS

Never be satisfied with mediocre faith.

Billy Joe Daugherty

Welcome . . . and honor men like [Epaphroditus], because he almost died for the work of Christ, risking his life to make up for the help you could not give me.

Philippians 2:29-30 NIV

You will never possess what you are unwilling to pursue.

Mike Murdock

I press on toward the goal for the prize of the upward call of God in Christ Jesus.

Philippians 3:14 NAS

A born-again Christian should be absolutely certain of where his power comes from.

Benson Idahosa

But you shall receive power–ability, efficiency and might–when the Holy Spirit has come upon you. . . .

Acts 1:8a AMP

Seek God first, and the things you want will seek you.

Anonymous

But seek ye first the kingdom of God, and his righteousness; and all these things shall be added unto you.

Matthew 6:33

. . . A miracle . . . is the tangible evidence of the supreme control of the Spirit of God over . . . materiality.

John G. Lake

And the Lord went before them by day in a pillar of a cloud, to lead them the way; and by night in a pillar of fire, to give them light; to go by day and night. . . .

Exodus 13:21

Faith moves first; then God moves in answer to faith.

Smith Wigglesworth

"Who touched me?" Jesus asked. Then the woman . . . fell at his feet . . . . Then he said to her, "Daughter, your faith has healed you. . . ."

Luke 8:45, 48 NIV

Faith looks beyond the walls of the obstacle and to the answer.

Benny Hinn

They went up on the roof and lowered [the paralytic] on his mat through the tiles into the middle of the crowd, right in front of Jesus. When Jesus saw their faith, he said, "Friend, your sins are forgiven."

Luke 5:18-20 NIV

Words . . .carry faith or fear, and they produce after their kind.

Charles Capps

Do not be deceived; God is not mocked: for whatsoever a man soweth, that shall he also reap.

Galatians 6:7

To live by faith . . . means that you don't look to [your] job as your source of supply.

Frederick K. C. Price

And God is able to make . . . (every favor and earthly blessing) come to you in abundance, so that you may always and under all circumstances and whatever the need, be self-sufficient–possessing enough to require no aid or support and furnished in abundance for every good work . . . .

2 Corinthians 9:8 AMP

Your faith begins where the will of God is known . . . .

Ray McCauley

In everything give thanks: for this is the will of God in Christ Jesus concerning you.

I Thessalonians 5:18

The gift of faith . . . comes on you and changes you into what God needs you to be at that moment.

Norvel Hayes

Then the Lord reached out his hand and touched my mouth and said to me, "Now, I have put my words in your mouth. See, today I appoint you over nations and kingdoms to uproot and tear down, to destroy and overthrow, to build and to plant."

Jeremiah 1:9

When the decision is right, you will know–God's perfect peace will rule in you.

Paul F. Crouch, Sr.

Let the peace of God rule in your hearts . . . .

Colossians 3:15a NIV

Simply take God at His Word.

Edwin Louis Cole

Abram believed the Lord, and he credited it to him as rightousness.

Genesis 15:6 NIV

You've got all the faith you need. Just use what you've got! Plant the faith you have, and . . . it will be increased.

Kenneth Hagin, Jr.

And the apostles said to the Lord, "Increase our faith!" And the Lord said, 'If you have faith like a mustard seed, you would say to this mulberry tree, 'Be uprooted and be planted in the sea'; and it would obey you.

Luke 17:5-6 NAS

Faith is able to look through the storm and see the end results.

Charles Capps

. . . "Only the ship will be destroyed. Last night an angel of the God whom I serve . . . said, "Do not be afraid, Paul. . . God has graciously given you the lives of all who sail with you.' . . . I have faith in God that it will happen just as he told me. . . ."

Acts 27:22-25 NIV

Remember that faith to move mountains always carries a pick.

Anonymous

For the Lord God helps Me, Therefore, I am not disgraced; Therefore, I have set my face like flint, And I know that I shall not be ashamed.

Isaiah 50:7 NAS

Faith is our sixth sense to contact the greater dimension of reality.

John Osteen

Suddenly an angel of the Lord appeared . . . .Peter followed him out of prison, but he had no idea that what the angel was doing was really happening; he thought he was seeing a vision.

Acts 12:7-9 NIV

Hope says, “I will get it sometime.” Faith says, “I have it now.”

E. W. Kenyon

And, behold, there came a leper and worshipped him, saying, Lord, if thou wilt, thou canst make me clean. And Jesus put forth his hand, and touched him, saying, I will; be thou clean. And immediately his leprosy was cleansed.

Matthew 8:2-3

Believe you receive in the faith realm, and you shall have it in the natural realm.

John Osteen

Then Jesus said to the centurion, "Go! It will be done just as you believed it would." And his servant was healed at that very hour.

Matthew 8:13 NIV

The power of faith is the ability to see that which does not exist.

Lester Sumrall

For He will give His angels . . . charge over you, to accompany and defend and preserve you in all your ways . . . .

Psalm 91:11

The moment you discover that there is power available to help you . . . you will see boundless opportunities to discover God's plan for . . . complete victory.

Benson Idahosa

"My grace is sufficient for you, for power is perfected in weakness." Most gladly, therefore, I will rather boast about my weaknesses, that the power of Christ may dwell in me. . . for when I am weak, then I am strong.

2 Corinthians 12:9-10 NAS

Thirty, sixty, and one hundred-fold blessing is indeed a glorious truth and blessing for those who will simply obey the Word of the Lord!

Paul F. Crouch, Sr.

Give, and it will be given to you. A good measure, pressed down, shaken together and running over, will be poured into your lap.

Luke 6:38 NIV

The power of . . . ministry [is] in [a person's] faithfulness, . . . integrity, . . . and willingness to serve.

Richard Exley

Then I said to them, "You see the trouble we are in: Jerusalem lies in ruins . . . Come, let us rebuild the wall of Jerusalem . . . ."

Nehemiah 2:17 NIV

If you believe God, He will move in your life.

T. D. Jakes

Wait for the Lord, and he will deliver you.

Proverbs 20:22b

Faith is not in miracles, but in Jesus Who makes them happen.

Reinhard Bonnke

". . . It is by the name of Jesus Christ of Nazareth . . . . Salvation is found in no one else, for there is no other name under heaven given to men by which we must be saved."

Acts 4:10-12 NIV

God's Word will stand the test.

Kenneth Hagin, Jr.

For the word of God is living and active and sharper than any two-edged sword, and piercing as far as the division of soul and spirit, of both joints and marrow, and able to judge the thoughts and intentions of the heart.

Hebrews 4:12 NAS

This is the first principle: Faith goes into the Word of God, believes God, and foresees as real fact what is not yet revealed to the five physical senses.

John Osteen

. . . People brought the sick into the streets and laid them on beds and mats so that at least Peter's shadow might fall on some of them as he passed by . . . and all of them were healed.

Acts 5:15-16 NIV

Faith means obedience. When you obey God, you have faith.

Norvel Hayes

During the night Paul had a vision . . . , "Come over to Macedonia and help us." After Paul had seen the vision, we got ready at once to leave for Macedonia, concluding that God had called us to preach the gospel to them.

Acts 16: 9-10 NIV

Trust God for your needs. Believe God for great things. Then receive great things from God.

Edwin Louis Cole

To him who is able to keep you from falling and to present you before his glorious presence without fault and with great joy— to the only God our Savior be glory . . . .

Jude 24 NIV

You have to give the very thing that you, yourself, need.

Paul F. Crouch, Sr.

A man reaps what he sows.
. . . . Whoever sows generoualy will also reap generously.

Galatians 6:7b;
2Corintians 9:6b

Faith . . . is the warranty deed that the thing for which you have fondly hoped is at last yours.

E. W. Kenyon

And this is the confidence that we have in him, that, if we ask any thing according to his will, he heareth us: And if we know that he hear us, whatsoever we ask, we know that we have the petitions that we desired of him.

I John 5:14-15

Whatever your situation . . ., set your eyes by faith on the Lord, . . . and continue looking until the tide turns in your favor.

Benson Idahosa

For we have no power to face this vast army that is attacking us. We do not know what to do, but our eyes are upon you.

2 Chronicles 20:12b NIV

Salvation comes as a result of an Abraham-type faith . . . based not on physical evidence but on the Word of God.

Kenneth E. Hagin

. . . If you confess with your mouth Jesus as Lord, and believe in your heart that God raised Him from the dead, you shall be saved; for with the heart man believes, resulting in right-eousness, and with the mouth he confesses, resulting in salvation.

Romans 10:9-10 NAS

[Faith is] the inner conviction of being overwhelmed by God.

Gustaf Aulen

Now Stephen, a man full of God's grace and power, did great wonders and miraculous signs among the people.

Acts 6:8 NIV

Praise lays the foundation for victory.

Rod Parsley

Enter into his gates with thanksgiving, and into his courts with praise: be thankful unto him, and bless his name.

Psalm 100:4

The Spirit can make His power felt in nature as well as through people.

John Wimber

. . . Paul and Silas were praying. . . Suddenly there was such a violent earthquake that the foundations of the prison were shaken.

Acts 16:25-26 NIV

Faith is a living, daring confidence in God's grace . . . so sure and certain that a man could stake his life on it a thousand times.

Martin Luther

The Lord is my rock, my fortress and my deliverer; . . . I call to the LORD, *who is worthy of praise, and I am saved from my enemies.*

2 Samuel 22:2-4

Life has no question that faith cannot answer.

Thomas L. Johns

Heaven is my throne, and the earth is my footstool. . . . Has not my hand made all these things . . . .?

Isaiah 66:1-2a

All authority is [illegible] Christ, so anything that He commands us to do, we have access to the power required to do it.

John Wimber

Then Jesus came to them and said, 'All authority in heaven and on earth has been given to me. Therefore go . . . .'

Matthew 28:18-19a NIV

A Psalm of Praise

But you'll realize with a freshness of heart,
and you'll realize then that the Spirit of God is not going to depart.
But He will sustain you and keep you by His power
because you're about to enter into your finest hour,
the finest hour for the Church to sing,
the finest hour to worship the King,
the finest hour to overcome,
the finest hour because the victory is already won.

Buddy Harrison

References

Unless otherwise indicated, all Scripture quotations are taken from the *King James Version* of the Bible.

Scripture quotations marked NIV are taken from the *Holy Bible, New International Version* ®. NIV ®.Copyright © 1973, 1978, 1984 by International Bible Society. Used by permission of Zondervan Publishing House. All rights reserved.

Scripture quotations marked AMP are taken from *The Amplified Bible. Old Testament copyright © 1965,* 1987 by Zondervan Corporation. New Testament copyright © 1958, 1987 by the Lockman Foundation. Used by permission.

Verses marked TLB are taken from *The Living Bible,* copyright © 1971. Used by permission of Tyndale House Publishers, Inc., Wheaton, Illinois 60189. All rights reserved.

Scripture quotations marked NAS are taken from the *New American Standard Bible.* Copyright © The Lockman Foundation 1960, 1962, 1963, 1968, 1971, 1972, 1973, 1975, 1977. Used by permission.

The Twentieth Century New Testament, text by Wescott and Hort. Copyright © 1904, Fleming H. Revell Co., New York.

Scripture quotation marked George Campbell are taken from *The Sacred Writings of the Apostles and Evangelists of Jesus Christ.* Copyright © 1974, Gospel Advocate Co., Nashville.

The Harrison House Vision

Proclaiming the truth and the power
Of the Gospel of Jesus Christ
With excellence;

Challenging Christians to
Live victoriously,
Grow spiritually,
Know God intimately.

Additional copies of this book are available
from your local bookstore or from:

P.O. Box 35035
Tulsa, Oklahoma 74153